D0929548

caffè ITALIA

caffè ITALIA

Indulge in Italian coffee culture at home with over 30 delicious recipes

Liz Franklin

photography by Peter Cassidy

RYLAND
PETERS
& SMALL

LONDON NEW YORK

Design and photographic art direction
Steve Painter
Senior Editor Clare Double
Production Manager Patricia Harrington
Art Director Leslie Harrington
Publishing Director Alison Starling

Food Stylist Tonia George
Prop Stylist Róisín Nield

Acknowledgments
A big bundle of thanks to the very talented team at RPS. Massive thanks also to Tonia for delicious food styling, to Róisín for finding the perfect props, and to Peter Cassidy for doing such a beautiful job of photographing it all. Thank you too for the continued support of my lovely friends, both here and in Italy. As always, I have been blessed with oceans of encouragement from my family—the most incredible Mum and Dad any daughter could wish for, two fantastic brothers and their families, and three amazing sons, Chris, Oli, and Tim. Words can't express just how grateful I am, how lucky I am, and how very much I love them.

First published in the United States in 2009 by Ryland Peters & Small
519 Broadway, 5th Floor
New York, NY 10012
www.rylandpeters.com

10 9 8 7 6 5 4 3 2 1

Text © Liz Franklin 2009
Design and photographs
© Ryland Peters & Small 2009

Library of Congress Cataloging-in-Publication Data
Franklin, Liz.
  Caffè Italia : indulge in Italian coffee culture at home with over 30 delicious recipes / Liz Franklin ; photography by Peter Cassidy. -- 1st U.S. ed.
       p. cm.
  Includes index.
  ISBN 978-1-84597-835-8
  1. Desserts. 2. Cookery, Italian. I. Title.
TX773.F727 2009
641.5945--dc22
                              2008040049

Printed in China

Notes
• All spoon measurements are level unless otherwise specified.
• Ovens should be preheated to the specified temperatures. All ovens work slightly differently. If using a fan-assisted oven, cooking times should be changed according to the manufacturer's instructions.
• All eggs are medium.
• All butter is salted.

contents

italian coffee culture & etiquette

Asking an Italian to contemplate life without coffee is almost as unthinkable as suggesting they might give up eating pasta—or expecting them to try and hold a conversation without using their hands.

To the Italians, coffee is more than just a drink; it's an institution, a way of life. In Italy, coffee-making is considered an art form, and it's one that's embedded in customs and traditions that stretch back for over 300 years. Whether you find yourself in the biggest city or the smallest town, the coffee or caffè bar is central to the inhabitants' existence. From the ornate buildings of old, with their hand-crafted wood paneling, gilded mirrors, and glasswork, to the slick and stylish avant-garde establishments, right down to the simplest village caffè, coffee is serious business; there's a way to make it, a way to present it, and a way to drink it. Quite simply, coffee is an Italian national treasure —and that's what makes the Italian coffee experience one that is still pretty hard to beat.

These days, Italians seem to have earned themselves a reputation for scurrying in and out of coffee bars like busy ants, stopping only for a quick caffeine kick before going about their business. That may be true during the work week—it isn't unusual for morning coffee to be taken en route to the office, ordered at the counter and drunk in seconds without even sitting down, but the Italians do still like to linger a little longer and socialize over coffee during their leisure time. Either way, it makes coffee bars lively and exciting places to be; for anyone traveling to Italy, no trip would be complete without taking in the caffè experience at least once.

With such pride and passion ingrained in Italian coffee culture, it comes as no surprise to find that enthusiasm for it has spread throughout the world. Where once many downtown cafés were run of the mill, existing largely to provide fuel stops for shoppers, now there is a growing breed of coffee shops that have followed the Italian example and become places to enjoy and appreciate first-class coffee; a focal point for relaxation, for meeting friends, and socializing. As a result, more and more of us have discovered the delights of good coffee.

Happily, the Italians have given us that skilled connoisseur of the coffee world, the barista. Barista comes from the Italian word for barman, used originally because many Italian coffee bars also serve alcoholic drinks and sometimes cocktails too, although the term is now generally taken to describe someone who is a specialist in making espresso-based drinks. Professional baristas are the sommeliers of the coffee world; adept in both the science and art of espresso making, paying attention to every detail from the complexities of bean varieties to grind variations and water temperature. Even the correct maintenance of the machinery is considered vital in the serious craft of coffee-making.

To get you started, here are a few basic pointers to drinking coffee in Italy

Caffè is the name of the drink and the establishment that serves it. Some caffès in Italy expect you to take a seat at a table, and a waiter or waitress will come to take your order. In others, you can choose to drink at the counter if you prefer. It

may mean that you pay a lower price, although it can be awkward if you have bags and you want to eat, unless juggling is your forte! In a number of places, you are expected to order and pay for your drinks first and then show the receipt to a separate person who will prepare them. This is often the case in busy large establishments and at railway stations, airports, and the (often very impressive) coffee bars at highway service stations. It guarantees people don't walk off without paying —and is good from a hygiene perspective too, because the person preparing the food and drinks doesn't handle the money as well.

When it comes to ordering, remember the short black coffee is called an espresso; an *expresso* is a very fast train.

Consider the cappuccino custom. Outside Italy, it's normal to see people sipping these frothy-topped coffees at all hours. Not so in Italy. It's a rare sight to see an Italian drinking a cappuccino after 11a.m. Why? Well, it's considered a breakfast drink, and is usually drunk first thing in the morning and accompanied by something sweet such as a cake or pastry. Italians feel that because it's milky and therefore quite filling, a cappuccino is a mini meal in itself. Sensible stuff if you think about it; after a typical Italian meal of several courses, there really

isn't much room at the end for a substantial cup of coffee. However, contrary to popular belief, you're unlikely to find that anyone actually laughs at you for ordering a cappuccino in the afternoon as we're sometimes led to believe; but you'll instantly give the game away that you're a *straniero* or foreigner!

A fairly common mistake is the use of the word latte, which is the nickname often given to a milky coffee without froth outside Italy. Well, latte means milk in Italian, so if you simply ask for a latte you're more likely to get a pitcher of milk than you are a coffee. Ask for caffellatte instead, and you should get what you're looking for.

Bringing it home

As we grow in our appreciation of fine coffee, it goes without saying that we want to take pleasure in the coffee we make at home, too. It is now easy to buy fantastic coffee-making appliances for the home, from simple stovetop moka pots to state-of-the-art espresso machines. On the following pages, you will discover how to make coffee in that wonderful, inimitable Italian way. Catch a little glimpse into the history of **Il Caffè Italia**—and learn how to create the best-loved cakes, cookies, and accompaniments that make the Italian coffee scene so special.

making great coffee at home

In order to make great coffee at home, it helps to understand a few basic principles about the coffee itself and the coffee-making equipment. It's no good investing in elaborate or expensive kit if you're using unsuitable beans or the wrong grind.

All the coffees mentioned in this book start with an espresso as the base. Espresso beans are usually roasted for slightly longer than other beans, so that they become dark and richly flavored as the oils they contain are drawn to the surface. Different coffee roasters make their own blends, and through experimenting you will find your own favorite. With any coffee, you'll get best results by grinding the beans just before using. There are two types of grinders, blade grinders and burr grinders (a good coffee shop will grind coffee for you, if you prefer).

Blade or burr?

Burr for sure. Blade grinders cut the beans using a high-speed rotating blade. The longer you run the machine, the finer the grounds become. The disadvantage is that the coffee grounds often end up uneven in size, which can make or break the quality of the coffee made in an espresso machine. The heat generated by the blades can also give the coffee a burnt, slightly acid flavor.

Burr grinders, on the other hand, crush the beans using a mechanism in which a rotating wheel, or burr, grinds against a static surface. This can be adjusted to regulate the size of the grind, giving a much more uniform result. There are two types; wheel burrs, which grind at a faster speed and can be a little noisy, or conical burrs, which are more expensive but are considered the best of all.

Getting the right texture

For good espresso, the grind is all-important; what's needed is a fine, slightly gritty texture that is even throughout. If the beans are fairly oily and the grind is too fine, an espresso machine will struggle to produce an even flow of liquid and you'll get a tentative trickle of coffee and no crema (the pale brown foam). If the grind is too coarse, you'll rush a torrent of water through the beans and again have no crema.

Cleaning and using your machine

For best results, keep your machine clean and descale it regularly according to the instructions.

When the machine is preheated and ready to use, run it with water for a few seconds before making your coffee. The head is best kept in place all the time, but a cold porta-filter will give you cold coffee. Warming it helps prevent clogging and also helps to keep the porta-filter at the same temperature as the water running through.

Storing beans

Exposure to heat, light, and air will cause any foodstuff containing volatile oils to deteriorate. For best results, store coffee beans in their foil pouch in the fridge or freezer, keeping the pouch airtight.

Espresso pod machines

For those who love good coffee but quake at the thought of getting the grind right or the tamp too light, these machines take small pods of vacuum-packed ground coffee and deliver the ideal dose of coffee, perfectly tamped. Depending on the model and the price you pay, they can make great coffee —but the cost per cup can be quite expensive, and the packaging does create extra waste.

The moka pot

The moka pot is common in Italian homes; it comes in varying sizes from tiny single-serving pots to those that can brew 12 cups. The moka pot doesn't make espresso, but does make reasonably good coffee at an affordable price, providing you take care with your choice of coffee and don't allow the pot to bubble on the heat for too long.

The base of the pot holds a chamber into which water is poured. The coffee grounds go into a filter which has a tube attached, and this sits on top of the chamber. The pot is heated on the stove and as it warms the steam pressure forces the hot water through the tube and into the coffee. From here it trickles into a top chamber, from which it is poured.

choose your caffè

Espresso An espresso is a short, very strong shot of coffee usually served in a porcelain demitasse cup known as a tazzina. In good establishments you should be offered a glass of water alongside it.

According to the Istituto Nazionale Espresso Italiano, the body founded in 1998 to safeguard and promote the espresso in the light of many poor imitations, the perfect example should always be prepared to order, made from ⅙–¼ oz. finely ground Arabica coffee, processed with 1 ounce water at 190°F and percolated for 30 seconds, and served in ⅔–1 ounce water (½–1 ounce south of Rome). It should have "hazel-brown to dark-brown foam, characterized by tawny reflexes, with a very fine texture, and should display an intense scent with notes of flowers, fruits, toasted bread, and chocolate. The flavor should be round but substantial and velvet-like, with well-balanced sour and bitter notes, but no taste of astringency."

If you want to order an espresso in Italy, ask for caffè; it will be taken for granted that you mean an espresso. If you would like a double, ask for caffè doppio (which is served in a larger porcelain cup known as a tazza).

Caffè ristretto Served in a tazzina, this is an ultra-short espresso made with less water than a normal espresso—for those who like a short, sharp knock-your-socks-off caffeine kick!

Caffè lungo For those who like espresso but prefer something a little less strong, caffè lungo is the answer. Extra water is run through the machine as the coffee is made and it is served in the larger tazza.

Caffè Americano Rarely drunk by Italians, caffè Americano is served in a tazza and is an espresso with hot water added after the coffee has been run through the machine. The result is a longer black coffee, typically weaker than caffè lungo.

Caffè macchiato Macchiare means "to stain" in Italian. So caffè macchiato is an espresso served in a tazzina with a "stain" of hot frothed milk that sits on the top. It's ideal for someone who enjoys a good short, strong coffee, but needs a drop of milk too.

Latte macchiato Just as a macchiato is coffee stained with milk, a latte macchiato is the reverse—milk stained with coffee. It is a long coffee, usually served in a heatproof glass or glass cup and is milkier and much less frothy than a cappuccino.

Caffè macchiato freddo Freddo means "cold" in Italian—so a caffè macchiato freddo is an espresso served in a tazzina with an accompanying pitcher of cold milk. In some establishments, a pitcher of cold milk is left on the bar so that customers can simply order caffè and add their own milk to taste.

Caffè corretto This is an espresso "corrected" with a shot of liqueur such as grappa, Strega, sambuca, or rum—just ask for your favorite.

Cappuccino All around the world, the frothy cup of cappuccino is perhaps the most famous and well-loved Italian coffee drink—the exception being in Italy, of course! The cappuccino takes its name from the Capuchin monks, an order of Franciscan friars whose hooded robes are of a similar color.

A cappuccino is traditionally made from espresso topped up with hot milk, which then has a layer of milk foam added at the end. It is served in the larger tazza. It's a general misconception that a cappuccino always comes with a sprinkling of chocolate powder on the top. This doesn't tend to happen in Italy, although it is often offered as an extra should you like it.

Caffellatte One part espresso, two parts milk, this is a milkier drink than a cappuccino, with less foam.

Caffè freddo The name usually given to iced coffee.

COOKIES & BISCOTTI

ricotta doughnuts *zeppole*

Zeppole are irresistible light ricotta doughnuts that are a snap to make at home. They are wonderful served warm from the pan, with a snowy shower of confectioners' sugar. The singular is zeppola, but I defy anyone to resist a second or third!

¾ cup plus 1 tablespoon all-purpose flour
2 teaspoons baking powder
a pinch of salt
3 tablespoons granulated sugar
8 oz. (1 cup) ricotta cheese
2 eggs
safflower oil, for deep frying
confectioners' sugar, for dusting

an electric deep-fat fryer

makes about 12

Sift the flour into a large bowl and add the baking powder, salt, and granulated sugar. Beat the ricotta and eggs together until smooth. Stir the ricotta mixture into the dry ingredients until thoroughly combined.

Heat the oil in a deep-fat fryer to 375°F. Drop several tablespoons of the batter into the hot oil at the same time. Fry the zeppole for 3–4 minutes, turning regularly, until they are puffed, fluffy and golden. Remove from the pan with a slotted spoon and drain on paper towels. Repeat until all the batter is used up. Dust liberally with confectioners' sugar. Serve warm.

butter sablés

In the caffès and pasticcerias of Italy, it is quite common to see these buttery cookies in various guises. Often, a little cocoa powder is added to some of the dough and it is then swirled into pinwheels or fashioned into little checkerboards. This basic recipe allows you to experiment for yourself using cookie cutters, or simply rolling the dough into a log shape and slicing it into discs.

basic sablé dough

2⅓ cups all-purpose flour
½ cup potato flour
¾ cup confectioners' sugar
15 tablespoons butter, cubed
1 egg white

cookie cutters (optional)
baking sheets

makes about 10

Preheat the oven to 350°F.

Put the two flours into a large bowl and add the confectioners' sugar. Rub in the butter until the mixture resembles fine bread crumbs. Add the egg white and draw the mixture up to make a soft but not sticky dough. If possible, wrap the dough in plastic wrap and leave it to firm up for 30 minutes.

Roll out the dough on a lightly floured work surface to a thickness of ½ inch and stamp out shapes with cookie cutters as desired (or cut with a sharp knife).

Arrange the biscuits on baking sheets and bake for 8–10 minutes, until golden. Remove from the oven and let cool for a few minutes. Transfer to a wire rack to cool completely and store in an airtight tin.

To make pinwheels Make the basic dough, then divide it in half and add 2 tablespoons cocoa powder to one half. Knead until the cocoa is incorporated and the dough an even color.

Roll out the 2 balls of dough on a lightly floured work surface to form equal-sized rectangles. With the longest side facing you, lay the chocolate dough over the plain dough and roll the two together as if you were making a jelly roll. Using a sharp knife, cut the dough into slices about ⅜ inch thick, and then arrange them on a baking sheet. Bake for 10 minutes, until golden and firm. Remove from the oven and let cool slightly, before turning out onto a wire rack to cool completely.

To make coconut sablés Make the basic dough and work in 2 tablespoons toasted desiccated coconut. Roll into a log about 1¼ inches in diameter. Spread 2 tablespoons toasted coconut over a sheet of parchment paper and roll the log through it to coat evenly. Cut into ⅜ inch slices and bake as the pinwheels.

cherry sablés *sablé con ciliegia*

Short biscuits topped with shiny glacé cherries (left) make a tempting offering with coffee. The Italians often use both red and green glacé cherries, but if you prefer to stick with just the red variety, they taste just as good!

6½ tablespoons butter, cubed

1 cup plus 1 tablespoon all-purpose flour

¼ cup sugar

2–3 drops pure vanilla extract

5 oz. glacé cherries

a nonstick baking sheet

makes about 10

Preheat the oven to 350°F.

Rub the butter and flour together until the mixture resembles bread crumbs. Stir in the sugar and vanilla and gather the mixture together to form a soft dough.

Break off little pieces the size of walnuts and form into balls. Arrange them on a nonstick baking sheet and push a glacé cherry into the top of each. Bake for about 8–10 minutes, until golden and crisp. Cool on a wire rack and store in an airtight tin until ready to serve.

almond and cherry cookies

These light and delicate little cookies are as delicious as they are pretty. You may need to add a little extra ground almonds to give a fairly stiff batter, depending on the volume of the egg white.

1½ cups (7½ oz.) ground almonds

1 cup confectioners' sugar

1 tablespoon potato flour

2 egg whites

about 20 glacé cherries

a piping bag and star tip nonstick baking sheets

makes 18–20

Preheat the oven to 350°F.

Put the ground almonds, confectioners' sugar, and potato flour in a large bowl. Stir in the egg whites. If the mixture seems a little too wet add a little more ground almonds until the mixture forms a fairly stiff (but still pipeable) dough.

Spoon the mixture into a piping bag fitted with a star tip and pipe little shell or fan shapes onto the baking sheets. Pop a cherry onto the narrower end of each cookie and bake for 5–6 minutes, until light golden. Let cool on the sheets for 5 minutes, before transferring to a wire rack to cool completely.

ladies' kisses *baci di dama*

My ladies' kisses biscuits have a delicious texture and an exquisite lingering flavor —just like the loveliest kind of kiss should have! To save time, I sometimes cheat and use Nutella for the filling.

6½ tablespoons butter, softened
½ cup caster sugar
⅔ cup ground almonds
¾ cup plus 1 tablespoon flour

chocolate butter filling
2 oz. dark chocolate, broken into pieces
4 teaspoons butter

baking sheets

makes 10

Preheat the oven to 350°F.

Beat the butter and sugar together until smooth. Work in the ground almonds and flour until the mixture forms a stiff dough. Break off 20 pieces the size of walnuts and form into balls. Arrange on baking sheets, leaving a little room between each. Bake in the preheated oven for 10 minutes, until golden. Remove from the oven and transfer to a wire rack to cool.

Meanwhile, melt the chocolate in a bowl set over a saucepan of gently simmering water (or microwave on full power for 1–2 minutes, stirring halfway through). Remove from the heat, stir in the butter, and let cool. When the cookies are cool, use the chocolate butter to sandwich them together.

toasted hazelnut florentines

Florentines are lovely with morning coffee, but make delicious petit fours to serve after dinner too—and they taste every bit as lovely as they look. Take care to be very precise with the measurements.

4 tablespoons butter

5 tablespoons sugar

1 tablespoon honey

½ cup flour

⅓ cup chopped mixed candied citrus peel

⅓ cup glacé cherries, finely chopped

⅓ cup toasted hazelnuts, finely chopped

1 teaspoon freshly squeezed lemon juice

1 tablespoon heavy cream

6½ oz. dark chocolate, broken into pieces

a baking sheet lined with baking parchment

makes about 15

Preheat the oven to 350°F.

Melt the butter, sugar, and honey together in a small saucepan over a gentle heat. Cool slightly and stir in the remaining ingredients except the chocolate.

Drop teaspoonfuls of the mixture onto the baking sheet, allowing a little room between each for spreading. Bake for 8–10 minutes, until golden. Let cool slightly and then transfer to a wire rack.

When the cookies are cold, melt the chocolate in a bowl set over a saucepan of gently simmering water (or microwave on full power for 1–2 minutes, stirring halfway through). Spread one side of each Florentine with a layer of chocolate and leave on the wire rack until set.

caramel almond cookies

These cookies consist of a crisp, buttery cookie base with a coating of flaky almonds in caramel. They are one of my favorites—and I think they make the perfect accompaniment to a mid-morning espresso.

cookie base

6 tablespoons butter, softened
⅓ cup confectioners' sugar
1 egg yolk
1 cup plus 2 tablespoons all-purpose flour

almond topping

4 tablespoons butter
½ cup granulated sugar
2 tablespoons honey
3–4 tablespoons toasted flaked almonds

a shallow baking pan, approx 8 x 12 inches

makes about 20

Preheat the oven to 350°F.

First make the cookie base. Cream the butter and confectioners' sugar together until smooth. Stir in the egg yolk. Work in the flour to form a soft dough and roll out on a lightly floured work surface to fit the baking pan. Lift it carefully into the pan.

To make the almond topping, put the butter in a small saucepan with the granulated sugar and honey and heat gently until the butter has melted and the sugar has dissolved. Bubble for 3–4 minutes until the mixture is golden. Stir in the flaked almonds. Spread the mixture evenly over the cookie base and bake for about 8 minutes, until the cookie base and topping are both golden. Let cool a little in the pan, and then cut into rectangles and transfer to a wire rack until completely cold. Store in an airtight tin.

tuscan soft almond cookies *ricciarelli*

I first tasted these soft almondy cookies in Siena, the beautiful Tuscan town where they first came from. Nowadays, these moist chewy cookies are a favorite all over Italy, and the delightful thing is that they're very easy to make at home.

8 oz. marzipan

½ cup granulated sugar

1 teaspoon Grand Marnier or other orange liqueur

1 egg white

1 cup blanched almonds, finely ground

confectioners' sugar, for dusting

a baking sheet

makes 16–18

Preheat the oven to 350°F.

Put the marzipan in a blender and process to a paste. Add the granulated sugar and Grand Marnier and process again. Transfer the paste to a bowl and beat in the egg white. Stir in the ground almonds.

Form the mixture into 16–18 small logs about ½ inch wide and 1⅜ inches long, and lay them out on a baking sheet, with room for spreading between each. Let stand in a cool place for 30 minutes, if possible.

Bake the cookies in the preheated oven for 8–10 minutes, until golden. Let cool a little on the baking sheet, and then transfer to a wire rack to cool completely. Dust with confectioners' sugar and serve.

LITTLE PASTRIES

individual apple tarts *crostatine di mele*

Little apple tarts are so quick and easy to make with frozen puff pastry dough. A little caffè I know makes a version with a layer of caramel under the apple, so I sometimes copy that, although I have to confess I cheat and use ready-made caramel (look for jars of *dulce de leche*).

12½ oz. frozen puff pastry dough, defrosted
4–5 apples
4–5 tablespoons honey

a 2½ inch biscuit cutter
baking sheets

makes 6

Preheat the oven to 400°F.

Roll out the dough on a lightly floured work surface. Cut out 6 circles about 2½ inches in diameter and prick the bases lightly with a fork. Lay them on baking sheets.

Peel and core the apples and cut them into very thin slices; arrange them neatly over the pastry so they overlap. Bake for 6–8 minutes, until golden.

Warm the honey in a small saucepan over a gentle heat and brush carefully over the apples. Serve the tarts warm or cold.

woodland fruit tartlets *crostatine ai frutti di bosco*

Fruit tartlets don't traditionally have a layer of chocolate covering the pastry, but it's a trick I use to create a barrier between the moist fruit and the pastry. The chocolate keeps the pastry crisp, even when the tarts are filled quite a way in advance. That said, the chocolate is a great touch anyway!

pastry

12 tablespoons butter, softened

¼ cup sugar

1 egg yolk

2 cups all-purpose flour

fruit filling

3½ oz. dark chocolate, broken into pieces

16 oz. mixed berries such as blackberries, black currants, and raspberries

½ jar blackberry jam

6 individual tartlet tins or a 9 inch tart tin with removable base

makes 6 tartlets or one 9 inch tart

Preheat the oven to 350°F.

First make the pastry. Beat the butter and sugar together until smooth. Add the egg yolk and beat again until thoroughly mixed. Stir in the flour and work the mixture lightly until it forms a smooth but not sticky dough. Divide the dough in half and freeze one portion to use later (see below).

Roll out the dough on a lightly floured work surface. Stamp out 6 circles using the tartlet tins as a guide and fit the pastry carefully into the tins. If time allows, chill in the fridge for 30 minutes, before baking for about 6 minutes, until the pastry is crisp and golden. If making the larger version, bake for about 10 minutes. Leave to cool.

Melt the chocolate in a small bowl set over a saucepan of gently simmering water (or microwave on full power for 1–2 minutes, stirring halfway through). Brush the chocolate over the base and sides of the pastry cases in a thin, even layer. Let set.

When the chocolate has set, fill the cases with the fruit. Push the jam through a fine strainer into a small saucepan and add 2 tablespoons water. Stir over a gentle heat until smooth. Let the jam cool slightly, and then carefully spoon it over the tartlets to lightly coat the fruit.

Note Pastry is easily made in a food processor. This recipe makes a double quantity, but with the egg it is impractical to make less. For a quick and easy pastry case, coarsely grate the frozen pastry into a tart tin and push down with your fingertips.

buttery jam tarts *sablé di marmellata*

If you don't have petit four-sized tart tins, simply break off walnut-sized pieces of dough, pop them on a baking sheet and push a finger gently into the center to make a well for the jam. Chill them for 30 minutes before baking if possible, because they may be inclined to spread a little—although they will still taste just as good!

1½ cups all-purpose flour
⅓ cup fine cornmeal
6½ tablespoons butter, cubed
¾ cup confectioners' sugar
2 egg yolks
4–5 tablespoons apricot or strawberry jam

2 x 12 cup petit four-sized tart tins or 2 baking sheets

makes about 18

Preheat the oven to 350°F.

Put the flour and cornmeal in a large bowl. Rub in the butter until the mixture resembles fine bread crumbs. Stir in the confectioners' sugar until evenly mixed.

Add the egg yolks and bring the mixture together to form a smooth dough. If it is a little sticky, dust with the tiniest bit of flour. Break off pieces the size of walnuts and push them into the tart tin cups. Use a tart tamper, if you have one, to mold the pastry into the tin, otherwise use a finger. Spoon the jam into the center of each tart. Chill in the fridge for 30 minutes before baking, if possible.

Bake the tarts in the preheated oven for about 10 minutes, until pale golden. Remove from the oven and let cool in the tins before turning out.

chocolate and almond tartlets *bocconotti*

These delicious chocolate and almond cakes are a specialty of the Abruzzo region. More often than not they have a pastry lid too, but I find them a little heavy on the pastry that way, so I make them as open tartlets. They are always very well received.

pastry
12 tablespoons butter, softened
⅓ cup granulated sugar
1 egg yolk
2 cups all-purpose flour

chocolate and almond filling
3½ oz. dark chocolate
⅓ cup ground almonds
¼ cup granulated sugar
1 egg white
confectioners' sugar, for dusting

a 2½ inch round pastry cutter
a 12 cup tartlet tin

makes 12

Preheat the oven to 350°F.

First make the pastry. Beat the butter and sugar together until smooth. Add the egg yolk and beat again until the egg has been fully incorporated. Stir in the flour and gather the mixture together to form a smooth but not sticky dough. Divide the dough in half and freeze one portion to use later (see note page 28).

Roll out the dough on a lightly floured work surface until it is about ⅟₁₆ inch thick, then stamp out 12 circles and press one gently into each cup in the tartlet tin.

Meanwhile, chop the chocolate into small nuggets and put them in a large mixing bowl. Add the ground almonds and sugar. Stir in the egg white.

Fill the tartlet cases with a spoonful of the mixture and transfer to the oven. Bake for 6–8 minutes, until the filling has set and the pastry is golden. Remove from the oven and let cool in the tin. Dust with confectioners' sugar and serve.

CAKES & TARTS

saffron ring cake *ciambella allo zafferano*

Ring cakes are popular all over Italy; the beauty of them is their simplicity. This pretty saffron-speckled version is one of my favorites, inspired by the fabulous saffron grown in L'Aquila in the region of Abruzzo, where I live. Using cream to provide the fat element in the cake gives it a lovely flavor, which combines superbly with the saffron, creating a delicate and delicious cake that is perfect with morning coffee.

1 cup whipping cream
a large pinch of saffron
3 eggs, beaten
2 cups self-rising flour
1¼ cups sugar
a pinch of salt

a ring mold, lightly buttered

serves 8

Preheat the oven to 350°F.

Pour the cream into a saucepan and add the saffron. Bring the mixture to simmering point, then turn off the heat and let the saffron infuse for 10 minutes.

Let the cream mixture cool and pour it into a large bowl. Whisk in the eggs, then add the flour, sugar, and salt and stir well until everything is thoroughly combined.

Spoon the mixture into the prepared mold and bake for about 40 minutes, until the cake is risen and golden and springs back when prodded gently with an index finger.

marmalade cake *torta con marmellata d'arance*

Italians use a lot of potato flour in cakes—it does help to give a lighter texture, but the result is sometimes a little dry. This cake traditionally has potato flour in it, but I make it without. It's the lovely combination of orange marmalade and butter cake that makes it so nice—and it looks pretty, too. If you have difficulty getting hold of cape gooseberries, little curls of blanched orange peel dipped in chocolate or dusted with sugar will also add a special touch.

12 tablespoons butter, softened

¾ cup plus 2 tablespoons granulated sugar

3 eggs, beaten

1⅓ cups self-rising flour

3½ oz. white chocolate, broken into pieces

12 cape gooseberries (ground cherries)

12 oz. orange marmalade

confectioners' sugar, for dusting

2 x 8 inch cake pans, lightly buttered and base-lined

serves 6–8

Preheat the oven to 350°F.

Beat the butter and sugar together until smooth. Add the eggs a little at a time until fully incorporated. Stir in the flour. Divide the mixture between the 2 prepared cake pans and bake for about 15 minutes, until springy and golden. Remove from the oven and let cool in the pans, before turning out onto a wire rack to cool completely.

Meanwhile, melt the chocolate in a bowl set over a saucepan of gently simmering water (or microwave on full power for 1–2 minutes, stirring halfway through). Dip the cape gooseberries into the chocolate and set on baking parchment to dry.

Sandwich the two cakes together with the marmalade. Dust the top with confectioners' sugar and arrange the fruit around the edge of the cake at regular intervals.

almond and pistachio cake
torta alle mandorle e pistacchi

A damp, delicious, and very dangerous cake, this, because it's hard to stop at just one slice. I suggest cutting the slices in half—then you won't feel so bad if you have two!

2 sticks (16 tablespoons) butter, softened

1 cup sugar

4 eggs, beaten

¾ cup ground almonds

⅔ cup ground pistachios

5 tablespoons plain flour

1 teaspoon baking powder

grated zest of 2 unwaxed lemons

pistachio topping

5 tablespoons sugar

freshly squeezed juice of 2 lemons

½ cup pistachios, chopped

a 9 x 5 x 3 inch loaf tin, lightly buttered and base-lined

serves 10–12

Preheat the oven to 350°F.

Beat the butter and sugar together until smooth. Add the eggs, a little at a time, and beat until fully incorporated.

Stir in the ground almonds and pistachios, the flour, the baking powder, and the lemon zest. Spoon the mixture into the prepared loaf tin and bake for about 45 minutes, until a skewer inserted into the center of the cake comes out clean. Remove from the oven.

Meanwhile, make the topping. Heat the sugar and lemon juice in a saucepan. Stir in the chopped pistachios. When the sugar has completely dissolved, pour the mixture evenly over the cake. Let cool in the tin and then turn out and serve cut into slices.

crumbly lemon cake *sbrisolona*

A gorgeous, lemony, crumbly-but-crunchy cake, which is a specialty of Ferrara in the north of Italy. Traditionally it is never cut, but simply broken into pieces to share. For fans of all things lemony, this cake should really carry a health warning because it is seriously addictive.

1 stick (8 tablespoons) butter, cubed
1⅓ cups all-purpose flour
½ cup plus 2 tablespoons sugar
¾ cup ground almonds
⅔ cup fine cornmeal
grated zest of 2 unwaxed lemons
2 egg yolks, beaten

a 9 inch springform pan, lightly buttered

serves 6–8

Preheat the oven to 350°F.

Rub the butter, flour, and sugar together until the mixture resembles fine bread crumbs. Stir in the ground almonds and cornmeal. Add the lemon zest and mix well.

Work in the egg yolks; at this point the mixture will become a little lumpy. Scatter the mixture evenly into the prepared springform pan, but do not press it down. Bake for about 45 minutes, until golden and firm. Remove from the oven and let cool, breaking into pieces to serve. To keep the Sbrisolona crunchy, it's best stored in an airtight tin.

rich chocolate and almond cake *torta caprese*

This is my version of an irresistibly rich chocolate cake that originally came from Capri, the island just off the tip of the Sorrento Peninsula. If they have caffès in heaven, I'm sure this must be on the menu. Serve in thin slices with a good espresso.

1 cup sugar

4 eggs, separated

13 tablespoons butter, melted and cooled

6½ oz. dark chocolate, finely chopped

1⅜ cups almonds, finely chopped

2 tablespoons Strega liqueur (optional)

confectioners' sugar, for dusting

a 9 inch springform pan, lightly buttered and base-lined

serves 8–10

Preheat the oven to 350°F.

Beat the sugar and egg yolks together until light and fluffy. Stir in the cooled melted butter and then the chocolate and almonds. Add the Strega at this point, if using.

In a clean bowl, whisk the egg whites until firm. Fold them lightly but thoroughly into the almond mixture until they are fully incorporated. Spoon the mixture into the prepared springform pan and bake for about 30 minutes (the cake will be slightly wiggly in the center). Remove from the oven and let cool in the tin.

Dust with confectioners' sugar and serve.

strawberry tart *crostata di fragole*

Beautiful tarts filled with glossy plump strawberries are a common sight in Italian caffès. They'll often have a layer of pastry cream (a rich eggy custard) underneath, as my version does, but if you're pressed for time, mascarpone is a simple alternative.

pastry

1½ sticks (12 tablespoons) butter, softened

¼ cup sugar

1 egg yolk

2 cups all-purpose flour

pastry cream

1¼ cups whole milk

¾ cup whipping cream

½ cup plus 1 tablespoon fine cornmeal

½ cup sugar

6 egg yolks

strawberry topping

16 oz. strawberries

½ jar good-quality strawberry jam (black currant jelly works well too)

a 9 inch tart tin with removable base

serves 6–8

Preheat the oven to 350°F.

First make the pastry. Beat the butter and sugar together until smooth. Add the egg yolk and beat again until thoroughly mixed. Stir in the flour and work the mixture lightly until it forms a smooth but not sticky dough. Divide the dough in half and freeze one portion to use later (see note page 28).

Roll out the dough on a lightly floured work surface and use to line the tart tin. Chill for 30 minutes. Bake for about 10 minutes, until firm and golden. Remove from the oven and let cool.

Meanwhile, make the pastry cream. Pour the milk and cream into a saucepan and heat gently. Combine the cornmeal, sugar, and egg yolks in a bowl and mix until smooth. Pour the hot milk mixture over the egg mixture, stirring all the time. Return the mixture to the saucepan and cook over a gentle heat until thickened, stirring constantly with a wire whisk. If there are any lumps, remove them with a hand blender.

Remove from the heat and let cool. To help prevent a skin forming, it's a good idea to cover the surface of the pastry cream with a circle of damp parchment paper. When the cream is completely cold, spoon it evenly into the pastry case.

Cut the strawberries in half lengthwise and arrange them neatly around the pastry case, with the thickest part of the strawberries pointing outwards. Strain the jam into a small saucepan with 2 tablespoons water and stir over a gentle heat until smooth. Let cool slightly, then carefully spoon it over the strawberries to coat the fruit lightly.

To make a jam tart Use two-thirds of the whole quantity of pastry to line the tin. Spread about 1¾ cups high-fruit jam over the base. Roll out the remaining pastry and cut into ⅜ inch strips. Arrange over the jam to form a lattice, lifting the strips carefully with a palette knife. Crimp them at the edges to seal. Bake for 25–30 minutes, until golden. Let cool in the tin.

chocolate and pear tart *crostata di pere e cioccolato*

A tart that is rich and fabulous and makes a wonderful treat with a good espresso. It also makes a fantastic dessert with a generous helping of vanilla ice cream.

pastry

1½ sticks (12 tablespoons) butter, softened

¼ cup sugar

1 egg yolk

2 cups all-purpose flour

chocolate and pear filling

14 tablespoons butter

1 cup sugar

3 eggs, beaten

1⅓ cups ground almonds

2 tablespoons flour

3½ oz. dark chocolate, melted

4 ripe but firm pears

sugar, for sprinkling

a 9 inch tart tin with removable base

serves 6–8

Preheat the oven to 350°F.

First make the pastry. Beat the butter and sugar together until smooth. Add the egg yolk and beat again until thoroughly mixed. Stir in the flour and work the mixture lightly until it forms a smooth but not sticky dough. Divide the dough in half and freeze one portion to use later (see note page 28).

Roll out the dough on a lightly floured work surface and use to line the tart tin. Chill for 30 minutes or so if time allows.

To make the filling, beat the butter and sugar together until light and fluffy. Add the eggs, ground almonds, and flour and beat until smooth. Stir in the chocolate. Spoon into the pastry case and smooth gently using a palette knife.

Peel the pears, cut them in half lengthwise and remove the cores. Cut them horizontally into ¼ inch slices and lay them evenly on the filling. Start in the center and fan them towards the crust to open out the slices a little. Bake the tart for about 45 minutes, or until the almond mixture is firm and the pastry is golden. Let cool, sprinkle with sugar, and serve.

coffee and chocolate tart *crostata al caffè e cioccolato*

Take care not to overcook the filling; you're aiming for a sort of fudgy, chocolate brownie texture. Kahlúa adds a distinctive, boozy, coffee kick to this tart, but you could substitute Tia Maria for a slightly sweeter result with hints of chocolate, or use any creamy liqueur. Reduce the quantity if using hard spirits such as brandy or rum.

pastry

1½ sticks (12 tablespoons) butter, softened

¼ cup sugar

1 egg yolk

2 cups plus 1 tablespoon all-purpose flour, sifted

coffee filling

1 stick (8 tablespoons) butter

1¼ cups muscovado sugar

2 tablespoons espresso beans, finely ground

6 tablespoons Kahlúa liqueur

2 eggs, lightly beaten

⅓ cup self-rising flour, sifted

to decorate

1½ oz. dark chocolate, broken into pieces

1 handful whole coffee beans

confectioners' sugar, for dusting (optional)

an 8 inch tart tin with removable base

serves 6–8

First make the pastry. Cream the butter and sugar together until light and fluffy. Add the egg yolk and stir until fully incorporated and smooth. Slowly add the flour and mix until the pastry forms a ball, taking care not to overwork the dough.

Divide the dough in half and freeze one portion to use later (see note page 28). Wrap the remaining pastry in plastic wrap and set it aside for 20 minutes. Roll out the pastry on a lightly floured work surface and use to line the tart tin. Refrigerate until needed.

Preheat the oven to 350°F while you make the filling.

Heat the butter and sugar together in a saucepan until melted. Add the ground espresso beans and Kahlúa, stir in the eggs, and then fold in the flour lightly but thoroughly. Pour the mixture into the chilled pastry case and cook for 20–25 minutes, checking after 20 minutes. Remove from the oven and cool.

Melt the chocolate in a small bowl set over a saucepan of gently simmering water (or microwave on full power for 1–2 minutes, stirring halfway through). Dip the whole coffee beans into the melted chocolate. Dust the top of the tart with confectioners' sugar, if wished, and arrange the chocolate beans in clusters around the edge of the tart.

ricotta tart *torta di ricotta*

There are so many versions of ricotta tart all over Italy, sometimes including pine nuts, sometimes with a lattice pastry top. My version is light, lemony, and lovely. I hope you agree!

pastry

1½ sticks (12 tablespoons) butter, softened

¼ cup sugar

1 egg yolk

2 cups all-purpose flour

ricotta filling

2 cups ricotta cheese

1 cup mascarpone cheese

1 cup sugar

3 eggs, beaten

grated zest and freshly squeezed juice of 2 large unwaxed lemons

confectioners' sugar, for dusting

a 9 inch tart tin with removable base

serves 6–8

First make the pastry. Beat the butter and sugar together until smooth. Add the egg yolk and beat again until thoroughly mixed. Stir in the flour and work the mixture lightly until it forms a smooth but not sticky dough. Divide the dough in half and freeze one portion to use later (see note page 28).

Roll out the dough on a lightly floured work surface and use to line the tart tin. Chill for 30 minutes if time allows.

Preheat the oven to 350°F while you make the filling.

Beat the ricotta and mascarpone together until very smooth and light. Add the sugar, eggs, and lemon juice and zest. Beat again until everything is thoroughly combined. Pour the mixture into the pastry case and bake for about 45 minutes until the filling is set. Remove from the oven and let cool in the tin. Dust with confectioners' sugar and serve.

cherry and almond tart *torta di ciliege e mandorle*

In May and June the south of Italy is bursting at the seams with cherries, so you'll very likely see a cherry tart or two if you visit then. This version is a stunner, with crisp pastry encasing a gorgeous frangipane filling, speckled with fresh cherries. See if you can resist a second slice.

pastry

1½ sticks (12 tablespoons) butter, softened

¼ cup sugar

1 egg yolk

2 cups all-purpose flour

cherry and almond filling

14 tablespoons butter, softened

1 cup sugar

3 eggs, beaten

1⅛ cups ground almonds

2 tablespoons flour

8 oz. fresh cherries, pitted

confectioners' sugar, for dusting

a 9 inch tart tin with removable base

serves 6–8

First make the pastry. Beat the butter and sugar together until smooth. Add the egg yolk and beat again until thoroughly mixed. Stir in the flour and work the mixture lightly until it forms a smooth but not sticky dough. Divide the dough in half and freeze one portion to use later (see note page 28).

Roll out the dough on a lightly floured work surface and use to line the tart tin. Chill for 30 minutes if time allows.

Preheat the oven to 350°F while you make the filling.

Beat the butter and sugar together until light and fluffy. Add the eggs, ground almonds, and flour and beat until smooth. Spoon into the prepared pastry case and smooth gently using a palette knife.

Gently push the cherries a little way into the almond mixture, distributing them evenly. Bake the tart for about 45 minutes, or until the almond mixture is golden and set.

Let cool and dust with confectioners' sugar before serving.

SAVORY BITES

hot chicken panini with artichoke pesto
panini caldi con pollo e salsa di carciofi

Warm ciabatta bread with a generous filling of hot chicken, oozing with an irresistible artichoke and almond pesto, is hard to beat for a tasty light lunch. The only accompaniment you need here is a good cup of coffee or a cool beer.

4 skinless chicken breasts

2 tablespoons extra virgin olive oil

4 small ciabatta breads

sea salt and freshly ground black pepper

artichoke pesto

1 jar artichokes in olive oil (about 6½ oz. drained weight)

½ cup finely grated Parmesan cheese

⅓ cup blanched almonds, finely ground

1 garlic clove

freshly squeezed juice of ½ lemon

3–4 tablespoons extra virgin olive oil

a ridged stovetop grill pan

serves 4

Preheat the oven to 400°F.

Beat the chicken breasts gently with a rolling pin or meat mallet until you have 4 thin escalopes. Brush each breast with olive oil and season with a little salt and freshly ground black pepper. Heat a ridged grill pan until hot and cook the chicken for 3 minutes or so on each side until cooked through (the time will depend on the thickness of the chicken). Put the ciabatta breads into the oven to warm.

Meanwhile, put the artichokes, Parmesan cheese, almonds, garlic, and lemon juice in a food processor and whiz to a paste (or mix using a hand blender). Add enough olive oil to make a smooth paste and season to taste with salt.

Remove the breads from the oven and cut in half. Spread the bottom half with a layer of artichoke pesto and top with a hot chicken breast. Pop the tops on and serve immediately.

Piadine are flatbreads, which are filled and then cooked in a padella (frying pan) until the filling is hot and melting. Large flour tortillas make a good substitute. It's worth roasting extra peppers to keep in the fridge to add to pizza toppings and salads.

arugula and taleggio piadine with pesto *piadine con rucola, taleggio, e pesto*

4 piadine or flour tortillas
10 oz. taleggio cheese, sliced
8–10 half-dried tomatoes
2 handfuls arugula
2–3 tablespoons extra virgin olive oil, for frying
sea salt and freshly ground black pepper

pesto
3 large handfuls fresh basil
2 garlic cloves, crushed
⅔ cup pine nuts
1 cup finely grated Parmesan cheese
3 tablespoons extra virgin olive oil

serves 2

To make the pesto, whiz the basil, garlic, pine nuts, and Parmesan together in a food processor, with enough olive oil to create a lightly textured paste. Season with a pinch of salt and set aside.

Lay 2 piadine on a clean work surface and spread each with a layer of pesto and taleggio slices. Scatter the tomatoes over and add a layer of arugula. Top each with another piadina.

Heat the oil in a frying pan and fry the piadine for 3 minutes or so on each side, until golden. Cut into wedges and serve immediately.

salami and roasted pepper piadine *piadine con salame e peperoni*

6 red bell peppers, seeded and thinly sliced
2 garlic cloves, thinly sliced
4 tablespoons extra virgin olive oil
4 piadine or flour tortillas
8 oz. salami Milano, thinly sliced
2 handfuls baby spinach leaves
2–3 tablespoons extra virgin olive oil, for frying
sea salt and freshly ground black pepper

serves 2

Preheat the oven to 400°F.

Put the pepper slices in a roasting pan. Add the garlic and half the oil and toss to evenly distribute the garlic and coat all the pepper strips in oil. Season with salt and freshly ground black pepper and roast for about 30 minutes, until softened and slightly charred. Remove from the oven.

Lay 2 piadine on a clean work surface and cover with salami. Scatter with an even layer of roasted peppers, then add a layer of spinach. Drizzle over any juices from the roasting pan and top each with another piadina.

Heat the oil in a frying pan and fry the piadine for 3 minutes or so on each side, until golden. Cut into wedges and serve immediately.

little cheese and tomato pizzas *pizzette margherita*

You wouldn't expect to find the same sort of hot-out-of-the-oven pizzas in a caffè as you would at a pizzeria, but you'll find smaller versions which have been freshly cooked that day—and they'll taste pretty special too. They're very easy to make at home and make a great light lunch as well as fabulous party food.

pizza crusts

3½ cups bread flour

1 envelope quick-acting yeast

1 teaspoon salt

1 tablespoon extra virgin olive oil

¾ cup plus 1 tablespoon warm water

pizza topping

3 tablespoons olive oil

1 onion, finely chopped

2 garlic cloves, crushed

14 oz. canned tomatoes

2 teaspoons sugar

small handful fresh basil, roughly torn (or ½ teaspoon dried oregano), plus extra to garnish

6½ oz. fresh mozzarella cheese

sea salt and freshly ground black pepper

2–3 tablespoons extra virgin olive oil, for drizzling

2 or 3 large baking sheets, sprinkled with flour

makes 6

First make the pizza crusts. Put the flour in a bowl and stir in the yeast. Add the salt and mix well. Stir in the olive oil and enough warm water to bring the dough together to a soft but not sticky dough. Sprinkle a thin layer of flour over a clean work surface and turn the dough onto it. Knead the dough for 5–10 minutes, until it is very smooth and elastic.

Divide the dough into 6 pieces. Roll each into a circle measuring 4 inches in diameter and lay on the floured baking sheets. Let rise for 40 minutes.

Meanwhile, preheat the oven to 425°F.

To make the topping, heat the olive oil in a saucepan and fry the onion and garlic over a gentle heat for 4–5 minutes, until softened but not colored. Stir in the tomatoes and the sugar, then season with a little salt and freshly ground black pepper. Bubble the sauce for 10–15 minutes until glossy and thick, then add the basil and let the mixture simmer gently for 5 minutes more. Remove from the heat.

Spread a thin layer of sauce across each pizza crust. Break the mozzarella into small nuggets and scatter over the pizza. Garnish with a little fresh basil and drizzle with extra virgin olive oil. Bake for about 8 minutes, until the cheese is melting and bubbling and the crusts are golden and crisp.

finger sandwiches *tramezzini misti*

It's said that these crustless sandwiches were invented at Harry's Bar in Venice, although they are found all over Italy. You can experiment with all kinds of fillings, but here are a few of my favorites. All recipes serve four.

prosciutto, pear, and arugula

1 small loaf white bread, sliced thick

3–4 tablespoons extra virgin olive oil

12 slices prosciutto di Parma

1 small ripe pear, peeled and sliced

2 small handfuls arugula

1 oz. Parmesan cheese shavings

1 tablespoon balsamic vinegar

Drizzle the bread with a little olive oil. Lay the prosciutto over half the bread slices.

Toss the pear, arugula, and cheese gently together with the remaining olive oil and the balsamic vinegar.

Top the prosciutto with a little of the pear mixture and sandwich together with the remaining bread slices. Trim off the crusts, cut into fingers and serve at once.

Note You could try San Daniele prosciutto instead of the Parma ham, or Grana Padano or an aged pecorino rather than Parmesan.

egg and asparagus

4 eggs

1 small bunch asparagus

4–5 tablespoons mayonnaise

grated zest of 1 unwaxed lemon

1 small bunch chives, chopped

1 small loaf white bread, sliced thick

sea salt and freshly ground black pepper

Cook the eggs until almost hard boiled. Leave until cold, remove the shells, and chop the eggs roughly.

Cook the asparagus in a large pan of boiling water for 2–3 minutes, until just soft. Remove from the water, cool, and chop into small pieces.

Mix the mayonnaise and lemon zest together. Fold in the asparagus, eggs, and chives and season with salt and pepper.

Spread the filling over half the bread slices and top with another slice. Gently trim off the crusts and cut the sandwiches into fingers. Serve at once.

crab mayonnaise and watercress

4–5 tablespoons mayonnaise

grated zest of 1 unwaxed lemon

8 oz. fresh backfin crab meat

1 small loaf white bread, sliced thick

2 handfuls watercress, trimmed

Mix the mayonnaise and lemon zest together. Turn the crab meat into a bowl and stir in enough of the lemon mayonnaise to bind it.

Spread the crab mixture over half of the slices and add a layer of watercress.

Place another slice of bread on each and gently trim off the crusts. Cut the sandwiches into fingers and serve at once (see left).

puff pastry ricotta and spinach rolls
salatini con ricotta e spinaci

Tiny and tasty, these savory rolls are made with the very typical Italian combination of spinach and ricotta. They are another Italian caffè favorite and often served in bars, as a snack with an aperitivo. Try the sausage version too.

16 oz. spinach leaves, trimmed and washed

5 oz. firm ricotta cheese

½ cup finely grated Parmesan or Grana Padano cheese

10 oz. frozen puff pastry dough, defrosted

1 egg beaten with
1 tablespoon milk

sea salt and freshly ground black pepper

baking sheets

makes about 24

Preheat the oven to 400°F.

Put the spinach in a saucepan with just the water that clings to the leaves after washing. Cook over a gentle heat for 2–3 minutes, until wilted and collapsed. Spoon the spinach into a colander, squeeze out any remaining moisture, then turn it out onto a board and chop it. Put it in a bowl and stir in the ricotta and Parmesan, then season to taste with salt and freshly ground black pepper.

Lay out the pastry on a lightly floured work surface and cut into 3 rectangular pieces measuring about 12 x 3 inches. Spoon a line of the filling all the way along the length of one piece of pastry, about the same thickness as a sausage and slightly off-center. Brush a little of the egg mixture along the narrower pastry border, then lift the other pastry edge over the filling to enclose it and seal the two edges together. Gently roll the whole thing over so that the seam sits underneath. Brush the top with the egg mixture. Repeat with the remaining pastry rectangles.

Cut each pastry roll into pieces about 1 inch in length and place on a baking sheet. Bake for 6–8 minutes, until puffed and golden. The rolls are best served freshly made and warm, but can be reheated if necessary.

To make puff pastry sausage rolls (*salatini con salsiccia*)
Follow the instructions as above, but substitute 14 oz. fresh Italian sausage meat for the spinach filling. Stir ½ teaspoon dried oregano into the sausage meat. Brush with the egg mixture and cook for 8–10 minutes, until the filling is cooked and the rolls are puffy and golden.

index

conversion chart

Volume equivalents:

American	Metric	Imperial
6 tbsp butter	85 g	3 oz.
7 tbsp butter	100 g	3½ oz.
1 stick butter	115 g	4 oz.
1 teaspoon	5 ml	
1 tablespoon	15 ml	
¼ cup	60 ml	2 fl.oz.
⅓ cup	75 ml	2½ fl.oz.
½ cup	125 ml	4 fl.oz.
⅔ cup	150 ml	5 fl.oz. (¼ pint)
¾ cup	175 ml	6 fl.oz.
1 cup	250 ml	8 fl.oz.

Oven temperatures:

180°C	(350°F)	Gas 4
190°C	(375°F)	Gas 5
200°C	(400°F)	Gas 6
220°C	(425°F)	Gas 8

Weight equivalents:

Imperial	Metric
1 oz.	30 g
2 oz.	55 g
3 oz.	85 g
3½ oz.	100 g
4 oz.	115 g
5 oz.	140 g
6 oz.	175 g
8 oz. (½ lb.)	225 g
9 oz.	250 g
10 oz.	280 g
11½ oz.	325 g
12 oz.	350 g
13 oz.	375 g
14 oz.	400 g
15 oz.	425 g
16 oz. (1 lb.)	450 g

Measurements:

Inches	Cm
¼ inch	0.5 cm
½ inch	1 cm
¾ inch	1.5 cm
1 inch	2.5 cm
2 inches	5 cm
3 inches	7 cm
4 inches	10 cm
5 inches	12 cm
6 inches	15 cm
7 inches	18 cm
8 inches	20 cm
9 inches	23 cm
10 inches	25 cm
11 inches	28 cm
12 inches	30 cm